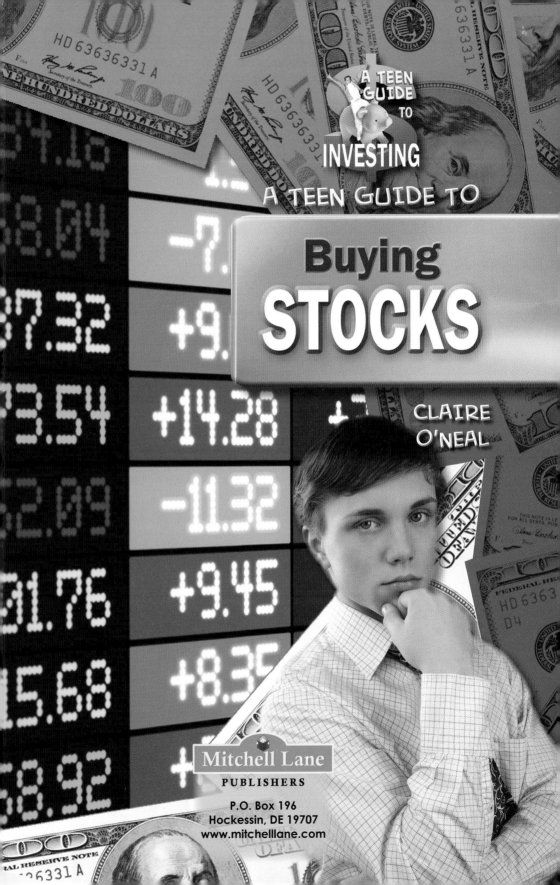

A TEEN GUIDE TO INVESTING

A TEEN GUIDE TO

Buying
STOCKS

CLAIRE
O'NEAL

Mitchell Lane
PUBLISHERS

P.O. Box 196
Hockessin, DE 19707
www.mitchelllane.com

A TEEN GUIDE TO INVESTING

Investment Options for Teens
A Teen Guide to Buying Stocks
A Dividend Stock Strategy for Teens
A Teen Guide to Buying Bonds
A Teen Guide to Buying Mutual Funds
A Teen Guide to Safe-Haven Savings

Copyright © 2014 by Mitchell Lane Publishers

Printing 1 2 3 4 5 6 7 8 9

Disclaimer: Mitchell Lane Publishers is not a securities advisor. The views here belong solely to the author and should not be used or considered as investment advice. Individuals must determine the suitability for their own situation and perform their own due diligence before making any investment. The publisher will not be liable for the results of any investments.

Library of Congress Cataloging-in-Publication Data
O'Neal, Claire.
 A teen guide to buying stocks / by Claire O'Neal.
     pages cm.—(A teen guide to investing)
 Includes bibliographical references and index.
 Audience: Grade 7 to 8.
 ISBN 978-1-61228-425-5 (library bound)
 1. Stocks—Juvenile literature. 2. Investments—Juvenile literature. 3. Finance, Personal—Juvenile literature. I. Title.
 HG4661.O535 2013
 332.63'22—dc23
                                                2013012371

eBook ISBN: 9781612284873

PLB

Contents

Chapter 1
Investing on Wall Street
5

Chapter 2
Buying Stocks in the Age of the Internet
13

Chapter 3
How to Pick a Winner
21

Chapter 4
Keeping Tabs on Your Portfolio
31

Chapter 5
Stock Strategy and Risks
37

Stocks to Explore
43

Further Reading
44

On the Internet
44

Works Consulted
45

Glossary
46

Index
47

The trading floor of the New York Stock Exchange

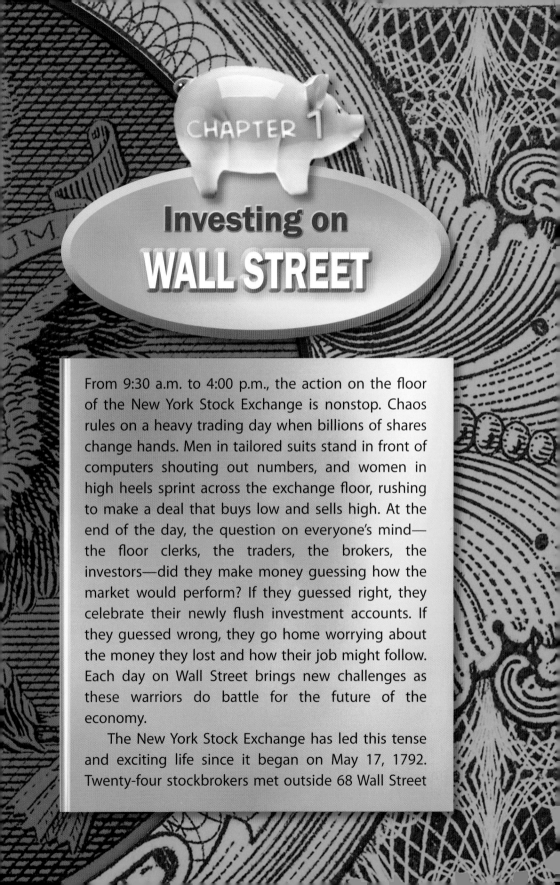

CHAPTER 1

Investing on
WALL STREET

From 9:30 a.m. to 4:00 p.m., the action on the floor of the New York Stock Exchange is nonstop. Chaos rules on a heavy trading day when billions of shares change hands. Men in tailored suits stand in front of computers shouting out numbers, and women in high heels sprint across the exchange floor, rushing to make a deal that buys low and sells high. At the end of the day, the question on everyone's mind—the floor clerks, the traders, the brokers, the investors—did they make money guessing how the market would perform? If they guessed right, they celebrate their newly flush investment accounts. If they guessed wrong, they go home worrying about the money they lost and how their job might follow. Each day on Wall Street brings new challenges as these warriors do battle for the future of the economy.

The New York Stock Exchange has led this tense and exciting life since it began on May 17, 1792. Twenty-four stockbrokers met outside 68 Wall Street

The Tontine Coffee House, at the corner of Wall Street and Water Street, served as New York's stock exchange building from 1793 until 1817.

under a buttonwood tree. They signed the Buttonwood Agreement, establishing rules for buying and selling shares, which are portions of a company that can be bought or sold. Shares would not be sold in private or in stores. Because corporations conduct their business out in public, the buying and selling of a company's shares needed to be done in public, too. The Buttonwood Agreement created a special marketplace just for selling shares, the New York Stock and Exchange Board, eventually known as the New York Stock Exchange (NYSE).

New York's stockbrokers were not the first to create a stock market. In order to sell shares to investors, the Dutch East India Company formed the Amsterdam Stock Exchange in 1602. The spices that the company's ships brought from Asia were in high demand in Amsterdam's shops. But for the businessmen who paid for the long sea voyage that brought them to town, these goods came at great financial risk, since ships and crews disappeared regularly along the dangerous route. The businessmen came up with an idea to make it easier on their pocketbooks. They would pony up part of the cash, and allow the public—especially the rich—to invest in their company. Investors paid the shipping company money to defray the cost of the voyage, but would later share the money made when ships returned loaded with exotic goods.

The Dutch East India Company's business model quickly spread throughout Europe, and investing soon played an important role in world history, including the beginnings of the United States. When explorer Peter Minuit bought the island of Manhattan from native tribes in 1626 for 60 guilders ($1,000 in today's US dollars), that money came from the Dutch West India Company. When Captain John Smith and his crew settled at Jamestown, they knew that all the land and any profits from it belonged to the investors of the Virginia Company of

The Dutch West India Company bought the island of Manhattan from the local Lenape tribe in exchange for a small trunk of goods.

London. History classes usually focus on leaders, colonies, and wars, but ignore the fact that the money to fund much of civilization's expansion for the past four hundred years has come, in one way or another, from a stock market.

Today, nearly every country with a large economy has a stock exchange of its own, from Saudi Arabia to Singapore to Chile. Asia and Europe hold most of the ten largest stock exchanges, including the Tokyo Stock Exchange in Japan; the Shanghai, Hong Kong, and Shenzhen Stock Exchanges in China; the London Stock Exchange; and Germany's Deutsche Börse. Canada's TMX Group is also a major player on the global scene. But no other stock market compares to those on New York City's Wall Street. The NYSE and the National Association of Securities Dealers Automated Quotation, or NASDAQ, are the two largest stock exchanges in the world. These two US-based exchanges alone traded $23.2 trillion worth of stock in 2012, more than the next eight largest world stock markets combined.

No longer just for shipping companies, stock today is traded for every kind of corporation in any kind of industry. Many of the things you eat, wear, play with, and use every day are made or sold by corporations traded publicly on a stock exchange. When you lace up your favorite pair of Nikes (NKE), eat a burger at McDonald's (MCD), play Guitar Hero (by Activision, ATVI), or ride in the car (General Motors, GM, and Shell Oil, RDS), you pay corporations money in exchange for something you want.

Your money helps the corporation succeed, but sometimes this money is not enough. Suppose a new company has lots of great ideas, but not much cash to support them. Amazon.com began with an idea in 1995; Jeff Bezos wanted to offer more books online than any bookstore ever could. Bezos could have gotten a loan from the bank to help Amazon.com expand. But Bezos doubted that his company would make a profit in its first five years. He would need to pay back a loan—with interest—during that time. Bezos instead raised money for Amazon.com through an initial public offering, or IPO, of stock. On May

Jeffrey Preston Bezos (b. 1964) grew Amazon.com from a dream in his garage into an international internet powerhouse, earning a personal fortune estimated at $25.2 billion along the way.

15, 1997, Amazon.com sold its first shares of stock for $18.00 per share. Eager stockholders bought a total of $54 million worth of Amazon.com. That money went into Amazon's bank account interest-free, and didn't have to be repaid. Amazon.com's IPO was a win-win for Bezos and for investors. In fact, if you had bought $10,000 worth of Amazon.com stock that first day, your investment would have been worth over $1 million fifteen years later!

If you are looking to make a quick buck, the stock market is probably not for you. The best place for money you'll need again within the next year or two is in a savings account. But over the long term, stocks have returned, on average, 10 percent per year for the last seventy-five years. They have blown away other investments like US Treasuries, with a 3.3 percent return, or corporate bonds, with a 4.5 percent return. Savings accounts offer even lower rates of return—as of 2013, some banks would pay you a dismal 0.1 percent interest on your money. Even 10

The New York Stock Exchange building at 18 Broad Street was designated as a National Historic Landmark in 1978.

percent may not sound like much, but thanks to the modern miracle of compounding interest, it can add up to big returns over time. In fact, young people actually stand to profit the most from the stock market because they naturally have an abundance of an investor's most important tool—time. For example, what if you could save just $1 every

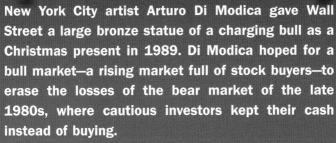

INVESTOR TRIVIA

New York City artist Arturo Di Modica gave Wall Street a large bronze statue of a charging bull as a Christmas present in 1989. Di Modica hoped for a bull market—a rising market full of stock buyers—to erase the losses of the bear market of the late 1980s, where cautious investors kept their cash instead of buying.

day of the year and invest that $365 in the stock market? Factoring in an average annual return of about 10 percent,* your savings would double in seven years and four months. That may sound like a long time to make an extra $365, but remember that your money grew without you lifting a finger for it. If you let your initial $365 sit in an investment account earning the same 10 percent for fifty years, it would grow to $42,848. That money is earned with very little effort on your part, leaving you with free time to earn even more money. So, what if you continued to save an additional $1 every day for each of those fifty years, and invested it all in the stock market? Over that entire time, you would have socked away $18,627. But after fifty years of compounding interest, that stash would be worth $510,157. Imagine what the future could hold if kids invested allowance money, or money earned doing odd jobs for family or neighbors like mowing lawns, babysitting, walking dogs, or raking leaves! It would be a rich future for kids indeed—if they knew how to invest in the stock market.

* Interest rates and fees discussed in this book are for illustration purposes only and may not be representative of actual rates or fees that are available at the time you are reading this book.

The very best time to start investing is when you are young.

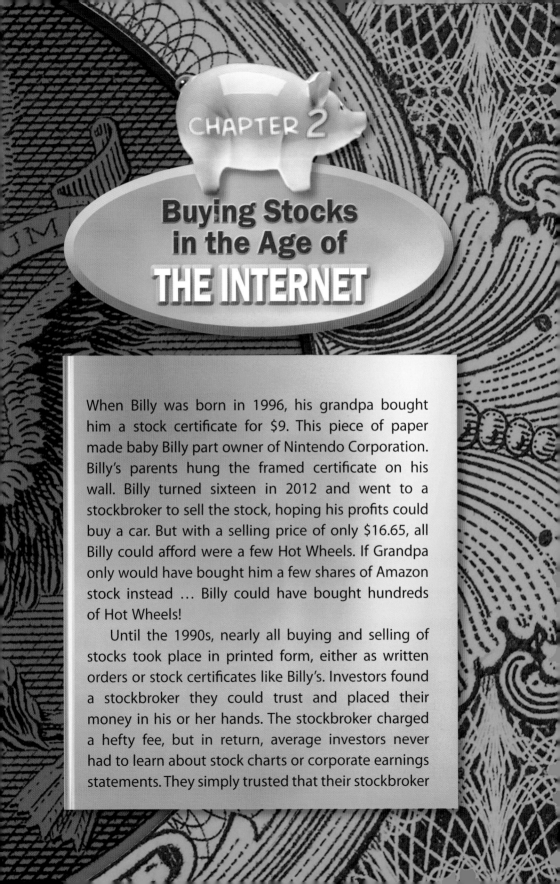

Buying Stocks in the Age of
THE INTERNET

When Billy was born in 1996, his grandpa bought him a stock certificate for $9. This piece of paper made baby Billy part owner of Nintendo Corporation. Billy's parents hung the framed certificate on his wall. Billy turned sixteen in 2012 and went to a stockbroker to sell the stock, hoping his profits could buy a car. But with a selling price of only $16.65, all Billy could afford were a few Hot Wheels. If Grandpa only would have bought him a few shares of Amazon stock instead … Billy could have bought hundreds of Hot Wheels!

Until the 1990s, nearly all buying and selling of stocks took place in printed form, either as written orders or stock certificates like Billy's. Investors found a stockbroker they could trust and placed their money in his or her hands. The stockbroker charged a hefty fee, but in return, average investors never had to learn about stock charts or corporate earnings statements. They simply trusted that their stockbroker

Stockbrokers are trained professionals. They must pass difficult exams through their state government and the Financial Industry Regulatory Authority to legally trade stock or give advice.

would buy and sell stocks using their money, somehow, mysteriously, making more of it.

Internet stockbrokers revolutionized the stock market in the late 1990s. Stock certificates and written orders, once the status quo, are today almost obsolete, replaced by the ease, speed, and accuracy of computer-based accounts. Though stockbrokers are still around to help investors who prefer a hands-off approach, the average trader today no longer needs one. Instead, potential investors can learn the ins and outs of trading themselves from research tools that are freely available at the click of a Google search, from how-to articles about the basics of buying and selling stocks, to news articles on investment strategies from top financial analysts. When ready, an investor can buy and sell for a small fee through websites of online brokerage firms, such as E*Trade, Scottrade, or Fidelity.

When is the right time to buy? When do you sell? The secret to successful investing is simple in theory: buy when the price is low, sell when the price is high. Supply and demand determines the price. Buyers pay more for stocks in high demand, such as Apple stock just before the company releases a new model of iPhone. But if buyers get bad news about a company—like when the Surgeon General announced that smoking cigarettes causes cancer—they won't pay as much for the same Phillip Morris stock as they did before. In reality, a stock's price is not determined by the company, but is simply an agreement between a seller with shares to sell and a buyer with money to invest. Almost anything that worries people affects a stock's price. Natural disasters and elections can cause the entire market to plummet, whereas an announcement that jobs increased nationwide could make the market soar.

Most investors buy common stock, which makes up the vast majority of shares offered on the stock market. Because shareholders own part of the company, they are usually eligible to vote in the company's annual meeting. Another kind of stock, preferred stock, is bought and sold exactly like common stock, but with one major difference. Preferred shareholders get paid before common stockholders, especially if the company goes bankrupt. Preferred stock may or may not give the stockholder voting rights. Some stocks, either common or preferred, pay dividends—company profits that are shared with investors. Dividends can be paid out in cash or in extra stock.

Your computer can put you in touch with a brokerage company, so get started researching the right one for you.

To buy stock, you place an order through your brokerage company, either in person or on the company's website. When you place a market order, you agree to buy shares of a stock at its current market price. For example, if you place a market order to buy ten shares of AT&T (T) stock, and T's current price was $34, your order would cost $340. If you didn't mind waiting, you could place a limit order to buy ten shares of AT&T when it reaches a better, lower price, like $30. Your limit order also specifies if it's good for just today, or until you say otherwise. If AT&T's stock price continues to rise, though, that limit order would never be filled. Stock is sold in much the same way. You can sell at the going market price, or you can place a limit order to sell when the price of the stock rises to a certain number. Some investors will also use stop-loss orders to sell stock if its market price drops below their comfort level. With this order, you can ensure that you won't lose more than a certain amount of money. But if the stock price later recovers and rallies to a new high, you risk missing out on potential profits by selling too soon.

Buyers and sellers can also place orders through options. An option is a contract to buy stock at a certain price. Say, for example, you wanted to buy shares of US Steel (X), currently trading at $22 per share. You think the price might go up, so you purchase a call option to buy one hundred shares at a price of $24 per share by a certain date. You don't own the stock—yet—you just own the right to buy the stock if

Just like a roll of the dice, you can never know from minute to minute whether the stocks you choose will make money or not. In the long term, your risk should pay off simply because stock values in general grow over time.

your conditions are met. The owner of the stock charges you a fee to set the contract, perhaps $2 per share, which in your case would be $200 total. Your brokerage will also charge a commission for handling your transaction. If the stock price reaches your strike price of $24, you can choose to buy the one hundred shares for that price, or $2,400. But you don't have to. What if you waited, and US Steel stock climbed to $30 per share? If your contract hasn't expired, you can buy the shares at the strike price, or $2,400, even though the stock is worth more. Selling the stock immediately would earn you $6 per share, or $600 (minus your $200 fee and broker's commission, of course). But what if US Steel stock drops and never reaches your strike price? Your contract expires, you never have to buy it, and you are only poorer by your $200 fee and broker's commission. If you believe a stock price will go down, you could buy a put option, which works much the same way, but for selling. Most investors stay away from options contracts because they can be confusing and very risky. But many professional stock investors use them to get maximum flexibility out of their investment dollars.

However you buy, hopefully you can sell your stock at a higher price than you originally paid for it. If you do, you'll owe taxes on these capital gains. Luckily, the government wants to encourage investors, since strong investments help boost the economy. You won't owe any taxes while you hold stocks. When you sell, capital gains from stocks enjoy favorable tax rates. Currently, capital gains on long-term investments are taxed at a maximum of 23.8 percent, which is less than the 25 percent or more many people pay in income tax. Lower-income investors may even be eligible to keep their capital gains tax-free. Tax rates favor dividends, too, also taxed at a maximum 23.8 percent. If you hold your stocks for less than a year, however, your short-term capital gains get no such break and are taxed at regular income tax rates. And if you had to sell your stocks at a loss, the government still helps you

Capital gains are profits made when an investor sells something at a higher price than he or she paid for it.

INVESTOR TRIVIA

Most stockbrokers are reputable professionals who pride themselves on helping their clients grow their money. However, horror stories abound of clients whose life savings disappeared in the hands of corrupt and greedy brokers. Bernie Madoff, one such infamous broker, led his own investment firm for over forty years. As the world became dominated by huge, impersonal online firms, Madoff and his sons maintained a private, trusted brokerage. Hollywood celebrities, charities, and Madoff's own friends loved how Madoff gave them steady returns on their money, even when the market was down. Perhaps they were too busy to care that Madoff didn't allow them access to their funds online, or that he was tight-lipped about the secrets to his success. In December 2008, Madoff's sons found out why the secrecy was necessary. Madoff only pretended that his client's returns came from investments. Instead, he stole new investors' money and gave it to his old customers, engineering the largest Ponzi scheme in US History. By the time Madoff pled guilty to eleven federal felony charges, his clients had lost as much as $65 billion.

out. Investors can decrease their tax bill by taking capital losses (maximum $3000.00) out of their regular income on their annual tax return. But remember that the government can change its tax laws at any time. Tax rates have gone up and down many times in US history. Before January 1, 2013, long-term capital gains and dividends were taxed at a maximum of 15 percent. With these new tax increases, some investors may alter their strategy, as stocks that offer dividends become less appealing.

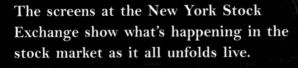

The screens at the New York Stock Exchange show what's happening in the stock market as it all unfolds live.

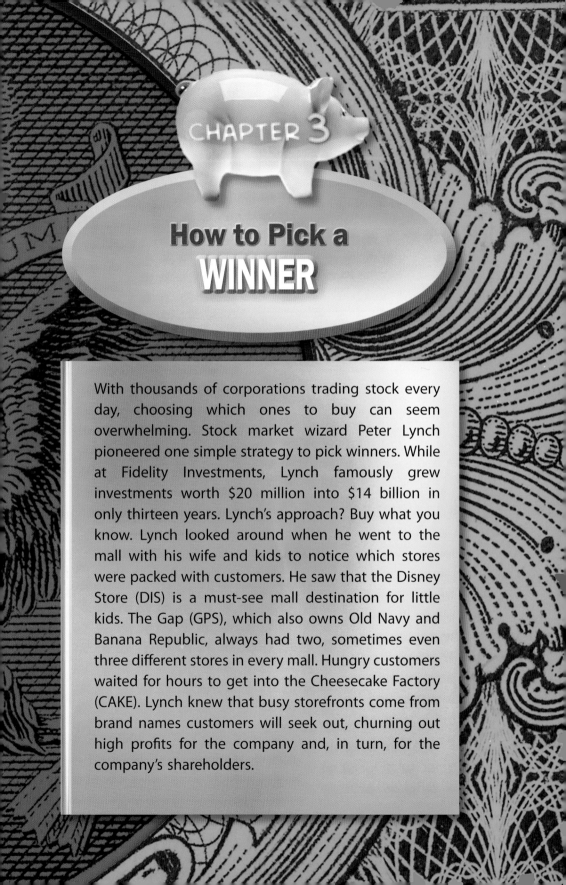

CHAPTER 3

How to Pick a
WINNER

With thousands of corporations trading stock every day, choosing which ones to buy can seem overwhelming. Stock market wizard Peter Lynch pioneered one simple strategy to pick winners. While at Fidelity Investments, Lynch famously grew investments worth $20 million into $14 billion in only thirteen years. Lynch's approach? Buy what you know. Lynch looked around when he went to the mall with his wife and kids to notice which stores were packed with customers. He saw that the Disney Store (DIS) is a must-see mall destination for little kids. The Gap (GPS), which also owns Old Navy and Banana Republic, always had two, sometimes even three different stores in every mall. Hungry customers waited for hours to get into the Cheesecake Factory (CAKE). Lynch knew that busy storefronts come from brand names customers will seek out, churning out high profits for the company and, in turn, for the company's shareholders.

Peter Lynch made a lot of money for a large number of Fidelity customers using a simple strategy: buy what you know.

Apply Lynch's approach to begin building your own collection of stocks, known as a portfolio. Not all companies offer shares of their stock to the general public, but many of the biggest ones do. Do you and your friends wear Nike (NKE) or Adidas (ADDYY)? Which system has the best games, Nintendo's Wii U (NTDOY) or Microsoft's Xbox (MSFT)? Do your parents buy their gas from Sunoco (SXL) or BP (BP)? Make a list of the companies you see winning the hard-earned dollars of your friends and family. It's a good bet that they are winning out in the stock market, too.

After narrowing down the stock market to a few choice buys, savvy investors get a better idea of the financial prospects of their stock picks through each corporation's annual report. The Securities and Exchange Commission, or SEC, requires every corporation that trades shares on the stock market to produce an annual report and make it publicly available. To help investors in between report deadlines, companies often announce predictions based on how business is going. A company that meets or exceeds its predictions builds investor confidence. But when a company's profits fall short, investors should question why, and whether it would be wise to sell. All of these reports and announcements are easy to find online with a simple Google search. In fact, let's look at Google's annual report as an example.

Each report begins with a letter from the company's CEO that sums up how the company performed over the past year and why. The CEO also lets investors in on business plans over the next year, dropping hints about new products or new business strategies to bring in higher profits. A CEO's job is to persuade investors to buy more shares in the company; he or she emphasizes the company's strong points and downplays, or even ignores, its weaknesses. CEO and co-founder Larry Page paints a lovely picture of how important creativity and long-term thinking is to Google in his 2012 letter to investors. But what investors will hone in on is Mr. Page's announcement of an upcoming two-for-

Google co-founder and CEO Larry Page (b. 1973) knew when he was twelve that he would grow up and start his own business. Today, Google.com is the most visited website in the world.

one stock split of Google.* In the near future, one share of Google stock, trading at $700 for example, will automatically become two shares, each worth $350. Though the total dollar value of all the shares remains the same, suddenly each shareholder owns twice as many Google shares as he did before. Two-for-one splits are the most common, but stock can split in any ratio, like 3-for-1, or even 3-for-2. Corporations usually split their stock when the price of a share becomes expensive, as Google's has. Shareholders will view a stock split as a confident move by Google's management, one that predicts even more growth in the future.

Next in the annual report comes the information stock pros really want to see—the income statement and balance sheet. Crafted by a company's accountants, these charts teem with enough numbers to make a math-o-phobe break out in a sweat. But pluck out just a few of those numbers and anyone can understand on a basic level whether or not a company is doing well financially, and whether it is worth your investment.

	Dec 30, 2011	Dec 30, 2010	Dec 30, 2009
Total Revenue	37,905,000	29,321,000	23,651,000
Cost of Revenue	13,188,000	10,417,000	8,844,000
Gross Profit	24,717,000	18,904,000	14,807,000
Research & Development	5,162,000	3,762,000	2,843,000
Selling General & Administrative	7,813,000	4,761,000	3,652,000
Total Operating Expenses	26,273,000	18,940,000	15,338,000
Operating Income	11,742,000	10,381,000	8,312,000
Non-operating income	--	-	--
Total Other Income/Expenses Net	584,000	415,000	69,000
Income Before Taxes	12,326,000	10,796,000	8,381,000
Income Tax Expense	2,589,000	2,291,000	1,861,000
Net Income	9,737,000	8,505,000	6,520,000
Preferred Stock & Adjustments	-	-	-
Net Income Applicable to Common Shares	9,737,000	8,505,000	6,520,000

Google 2011 Income Statement from Yahoo Finance

* http://investor.google.com/corporate/2012/founders-letter.html

	2011	2010	2009
Assets			
Cash and Cash Equivalents	9.983,000	13,630,000	10,198,000
Short-Term Investments	34,643,000	21,345,000	14,287,000
Accounts Receivable	6,387,000	5,261,000	3,845,000
Other Current Assets	1,745,000	1,326,000	837,000
Total Current Assets	52,758,000	41,562,000	29,167,000
Property, Plant, and Equipment	9,603,000	7,759,000	4,845,000
Long-term Investments	790,000	523,000	129,000
Other Long-Term Assets	9,423,000	8,007,000	6,356,000
Total Non-Current Assets	19,816,000	16,289,000	11,300,000
Total Assets	72,574,000	57,851,000	40,497,000
Liabilities			
Accounts Payable	7,148,000	6,137,000	2,462,000
Short Term Debt	1,218,000	3,465,000	–
Other Current Liabilities	547,000	394,000	285,000
Total Current Liabilities	8,913,000	9,996,000	2,747,000
Long Term Debt	2,986,000	–	–
Other Long-Term Liabilities	2,530,000	1,614,000	1,746,000
Total Non-Current Liabilities	5,516,000	1,614,000	1,746,000
Total Liabilities	14,429,000	11,610,000	4,493,000
Stockholders' Equity			
Common Stock	20,264,000	18,235,000	15,817,000
Retained Earnings & Other Equity	37,881,000	28,006,000	20,187,000
Total Stockholder Equity	58,145,000	46,241,000	36,004,000

Google 2011 Balance Sheet. Accessed from Yahoo! Finance (http://finance.yahoo.com/q?s=GOOG)

The income statement describes, with numbers, how a company performed financially over a period of time. In the annual report, the period is one year. The SEC also requires companies to file a quarterly statement for each financial quarter, or three-month period. For a quick look, focus on the company's *total expenses*—the cost of doing its business—and its *net income*—how much profit the company made after all its bills were paid. For three years running, Google's net income rose, the hallmark of a successful company. Investors generally like to see expenses go down over time. Google's do not, and in fact, it continually spends more to do business every year. But having read the CEO's letter, investors know that this spending is a good thing, intended to help Google grow and develop as a corporation.

A company's balance sheet lays bare its assets and liabilities for investors to see. Assets include the company's cash, property, and money it is owed. When business is good, assets increase. Liabilities represent the money that a company owes, like rent, salaries, cost of materials to make a product, taxes, loans, and more. Shareholders' equity is spelled out on the balance sheet as whatever assets are not canceled out by the company's liabilities. In fact, this relationship is what makes a balance sheet balance: shareholders' equity = assets – liabilities.

One look at Google's balance sheet and you can see that its business is booming. Successful companies have more assets than liabilities. Google's assets not only outweigh its liabilities, but have also grown steadily over the past three years. On the other hand, a company with lots of liabilities may turn out to be a good investment in the long run, but in the near future it is a riskier investment. If a company goes bankrupt, investors who own its stock risk losing their entire investment. Comparing financial statements between different companies in the same industry, such as Google with Yahoo! Inc, is a useful strategy to see which one would be the better buy.

As the Latin saying goes, *caveat emptor,* or buyer beware. Some companies use their financial statements to trick investors. In 2000, Enron, an energy company based in Houston, Texas, claimed over $100 billion in income. As a rising star and a new darling of the stock market, Enron neglected to mention on its balance sheet how its ownership of lots of smaller energy businesses actually meant it was swimming in debt. When Enron's accounting schemes were uncovered, its stock price plummeted from $83 per share in December 2000, to less than $1 in November 2001. Enron quickly went out of business. The company held the record for the largest bankruptcy in US history, until the next year when the SEC caught telecommunications giant WorldCom in a

This skyscraper at 1400 Smith Street in downtown Houston, Texas was once the headquarters for the Enron Corporation.

similar act. Investors who had read Enron and WorldCom's annual reports with a careful eye stood a chance of selling their stock before they lost their shirts.

Google looks great for now. But don't rush out and spend all your allowance buying only that stock. What if a natural disaster hit Google's headquarters tomorrow and destroyed its equipment? Google's stock could tumble and its investors would lose their money. To ensure yourself a truly healthy financial future, you must diversify. Savvy investors buy not just one type of stock, but a whole portfolio. Some analysts advise investors to keep 10 percent of their money or less in a single stock. Buy shares in a variety of different companies in different industries—not just technology, but health care, energy, utilities, materials, consumer goods, industrial goods, services, and financial corporations. The more diverse a portfolio, the less risk it carries of losing money.

Another way to add diversity is to buy stock in companies of different sizes. Investors determine a company's size from its market

Ann Taylor, a women's clothing retailer.

capitalization, or the total value of its stock on the market. Most companies start as "small caps" when they go public, with market caps of less than $2 billion. Small caps can stay small to serve a specialized clientele, such as Ann Taylor clothing stores (ANN, market cap 1.36B). Others aim to grow. When business takes off, the price of a small cap's stock rises. The corporation can then raise more money to grow faster—building more factories or hiring better people—by making more stock available for investors to buy. This larger number, or volume, of shares trading, combined with higher per-share prices, pushes the company into the mid-cap range. Mid-cap stocks claim a market share of between $2 billion and $10 billion. They feel just right to some investors—not too big and not too small. Growing mid caps include CarMax (KMX, market cap 9.04B) and video game maker Electronic Arts, Inc. (EA, market cap 5.22B), but once-large corporations on their way down can also trade as mid caps. Large-cap stocks have a minimum market cap of $10 billion, and tend to be huge, established, multinational corporations. Many large-cap stocks are household names, like John Deere (DE, market cap 36.16B) and Visa (V, market cap 103.40B). Blue-chip stocks form an elite category of large-cap corporations that show consistent financial performance. Investors count on these leaders in their industry, like The Home Depot (HD) and General Electric (GE), to turn a steady profit in good times and bad. Conservative investors prefer blue chips for their slow but steady growth and low risk. It's unlikely that an enormous company will go bankrupt anytime soon. On the other hand, aggressive investors who want their money to grow fast, and don't mind a little risk, might cherry-pick small-cap stocks from innovative companies that could be the next big thing.

A very popular investing strategy among America's workers today is dollar-cost averaging, or buying stock systematically over time. Many working men and women invest money through their company's retirement plan, sometimes known as a 401(k). Part of each paycheck goes directly into an investment account to help the employee save for retirement. Just like how you invested $1 a day in Chapter 1, investing this way makes the stock market more affordable, since investors build their wealth a little at a time. It also gives the investor instant portfolio diversity in another way—not in stocks, but *in time*. If share prices drop, the value of a 401(k) might go down in the short term, but investors benefit in the long run from buying when prices are low. The biggest risk comes in timing their retirement. If an investor cashes in his 401k during a bear market, he stands to lose at least some, if not all, of his investment.

A newspaper may just
play a big part in your
investment strategy.

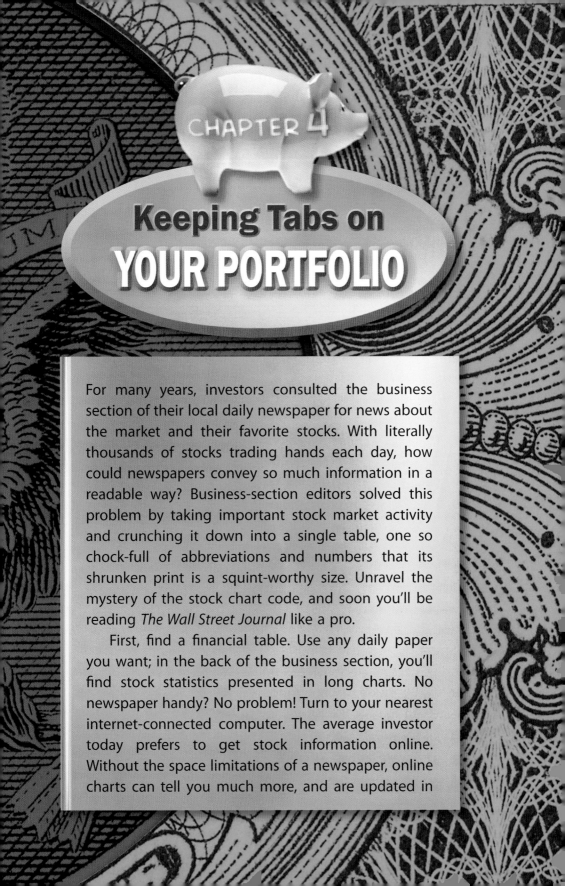

CHAPTER 4

Keeping Tabs on
YOUR PORTFOLIO

For many years, investors consulted the business section of their local daily newspaper for news about the market and their favorite stocks. With literally thousands of stocks trading hands each day, how could newspapers convey so much information in a readable way? Business-section editors solved this problem by taking important stock market activity and crunching it down into a single table, one so chock-full of abbreviations and numbers that its shrunken print is a squint-worthy size. Unravel the mystery of the stock chart code, and soon you'll be reading *The Wall Street Journal* like a pro.

First, find a financial table. Use any daily paper you want; in the back of the business section, you'll find stock statistics presented in long charts. No newspaper handy? No problem! Turn to your nearest internet-connected computer. The average investor today prefers to get stock information online. Without the space limitations of a newspaper, online charts can tell you much more, and are updated in

INVESTOR TRIVIA

Edward Calahan invented the stock ticker in 1863 to send stock quotes from the exchange floor to investors nationwide using a telegraph machine. The ticking sound of the telegraph printer gave the invention its name. Today, a "stock ticker" is any device that reports instant changes in stock prices.

real time throughout the day's trading. Just type the company's name in search engines like Google or Yahoo!, or visit the website of an online investment firm like Charles Schwab or Ameritrade. Newspaper readers have to wait until tomorrow to read the same statistics you can get instantly online.

Let's explore the financial tables using an investing example. Perhaps you like Coke, but your friend likes Pepsi. You both want to invest in your favorite brand of bubbly goodness. Who will make more money? Locate each corporation by its ticker symbol. This assigned abbreviation, usually two to five letters long, is easier to display than the company's full name. Some ticker symbols are obvious, like McDonald's (symbol: MCD), Facebook (FB), or Caterpillar (CAT). Others translate from a much longer corporate name, like Shell Oil (formally known as Royal Dutch Shell, or RDS), or the parent company that owns KFC and Pizza Hut (Yum! Brands, or YUM). Still others show that even Wall Street has a sense of humor, like Papa John's International (PZZA), or Market Vectors Agribusiness (MOO). The Coca-Cola Company trades under KO; PepsiCo's ticker symbol is PEP.

Pretend today is Monday, March 25, 2013, and markets are open and trading away. "Open 40.11" tells you that KO traded for $40.11 per share when the markets opened at 9:30 a.m. "Prev Close 40.04" means that KO traded for $40.04 per share when the markets closed for the day on Friday at 4:00 p.m. Right now, KO is trading at a market value of $40.16, up $0.12 from 9:30 a.m., a 0.29 percent change (0.29%). But these prices don't tell the whole story. After all, "Mkt Cap" shows that the enormous Coca-Cola Company has a market cap of 179.03B ($179,030,000,000). In fact, Coca-Cola is one of the blue-chip components of the Dow Jones Industrial Average. Traders right now are buying and selling nearly 15 million shares of KO during trading today, at prices ranging from $40.25 to $40.01 ("Day's Range"). Even over the past fifty-two weeks, or one year, KO's price fluctuated between a low of $35.58 and a high of $40.67 ("52wk Range").

Now, compare this to PepsiCo. Its current trading price, $78.00, is higher. You could buy nearly two shares of KO for every one share your friend buys of PEP. But which company's stock offers the biggest bang for your buck right now? We'll use three stats—EPS, P/E, and Div/ Yield%—to find out.

The Coca-Cola Company (KO) - NYSE

40.16 ↑0.12(0.29%) 11:55AM EDT - Nasdaq Real Time Price

➕ Add to Portfolio   ◼ Like   433

Prev Close:	40.04	Day's Range:	40.01 - 40.25
Open:	40.11	52wk Range:	35.58 - 40.67
Bid:	40.17 x 5300	Volume:	6,190,207
Ask:	40.18 x 3200	Avg Vol (3m):	14,980,000
1y Target Est:	42.46	Market Cap:	179.03B
Beta:	0.38	P/E (ttm):	20.40
Next Earnings Date:	16-Apr-13 📅	EPS (ttm):	1.97
		Div & Yield:	1.12 (2.80%)

Coca-Cola Company (The) Common
◼ KO

40.25
40.20
40.15
40.10
40.05
40.00

© Yahoo!
10am   12pm   2pm   4pm
------ Previous Close

1d 5d 1m 3m 6m 1y 2y 5y max

Online charts provide all the stats you'll need to keep tabs on the stock of your favorite beverage company.

Coke vs. Pepsi

Coke, Pepsi bottler deals to boost long-term profits

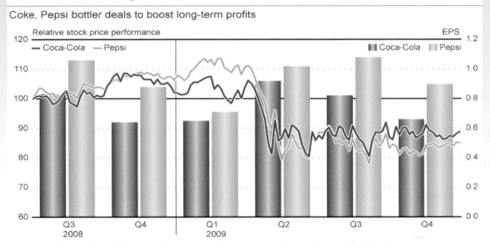

Coke (blue) and Pepsi (orange) ran neck-and-neck during 2008 and 2009 in their earnings-per-share (bars) as well as their stock price (lines). (Coke rewarded its shareholders with a two-for-one split in July 2012.)

The "EPS," or earnings per share, tells you how much money a single share has earned over time, usually over the past year. You can calculate an EPS on your own; simply divide a company's net income (as reported on its income statement) by the number of its shares available for trade. Comparing EPS of two stocks in the same industry gives you an idea of which is the smarter buy. KO's EPS checks in at $1.97 today. Investors in PepsiCo earned almost twice as much per share over the past year, with an EPS of $3.92. Remember, however, that Coke's stock is cheaper. If you bought two of its shares, you would have spent only a little more than your friend, and you would have earned $3.94 over the past year. No clear winner there. But let's say you wanted to buy Google stock and your friend bought Apple. Both stocks are expensive, but also have a reputation as big money makers. Google's EPS is a whopping $32.21. But this time your friend wins; Apple's EPS cha-chings in at $44.11.

Back to the epic battle of Coke versus Pepsi. Another clue to a stock's outlook is "P/E," which stands for price-to-earnings ratio. The P/E ratio, calculated by dividing the current share price by the stock's EPS, tells you how much investors are willing to pay today to make $1 a year using this stock. On March 25, Coca-Cola's P/E ratio was 20.39, meaning that investors at that time were paying $20.39 to grow an extra buck. Compare that to PepsiCo's P/E ratio on the same day, 19.86. Another way to look at it: if you divide 1 by the P/E ratio—1/20.39—you get the earnings yield, in Coke's case, 4.9 percent. Pepsi's yield is just a bit higher, at 5.04 percent. So, even though PepsiCo's stock is more expensive, it's a slightly cheaper way to make money.

Fans of dividend stocks seek out Div/Yield%, which reports how much dividend the corporation paid per share ("Div"), and how this adds to an investor's annual returns ("Yield%"). KO stock paid investors $1.12 per share ("Div"). Over the past year, Coke's returns to investors paid out 2.80 percent of the stock's current price in dividends. This may not sound like much, but it beats average savings account yields of less than 1 percent per year, hands down. In contrast, PepsiCo paid a dividend of $2.15 per share this year, a yield of 2.70 percent. Looks like Pepsi and Coke do taste almost the same … at least to investors in today's stock market.

INVESTOR TRIVIA

Funny stock symbols
Avis Car Rental—CAR
Dynamic Materials Corporation—BOOM
Asia Tigers Fund—GRR
Southwest Airlines—LUV
Harley-Davidson—HOG
Cedar Fair (amusement parks)—FUN
PowerShares Dynamic Food & Beverage—PBJ
First Trust Global Wind Energy—FAN
Guggenheim Solar—TAN

Presidential Medal of Freedom winner Warren Buffett discusses the economy with President Barack Obama at the White House in 2010.

CHAPTER 5

Stock Strategy
AND RISKS

Warren Buffett lives in a modest home in Omaha, Nebraska, wears sensible shoes, and eats at McDonald's. Buffett bought his first stock when he was eleven—three shares of Cities Service preferred stock at $38 per share. Soon after, the stock dropped to $27. Buffett held on, and soon sold his stock at $40 per share, a $6 profit. But when Cities Service stock rose to almost $200 per share, Buffett learned a humbling lesson in patience. Today, Buffett has a zen-like patience when it comes to selling stock. He is famous for saying that his "favorite holding period is forever." The eighty-two-year-old investor also sits on the third-largest personal fortune in the world, valued at $53.5 billion.

Buffett makes no secret of the value-investing approach he pioneered through his investment firm, Berkshire Hathaway. Like a bargain hunter at Wal-Mart, Buffett has a special talent for spotting undervalued stocks, ones with below-average P/E ratios. The S&P 500 has a historic average P/E of 15;

value investors seek out stocks with lower P/Es. Buffett also insists on buying stock in companies with products or services that anyone can understand, like American Express or Gillette.

Growth investors do exactly the opposite, hunting for stocks from young successful companies that look to become even more successful. Thomas Rowe Price Jr. looked for companies that had an edge over close competitors, like Proctor & Gamble (PG) and IBM (IBM). In 1965, his funds earned a 44 percent gain, compared to the S&P 500's paltry 12 percent.

Like all investors in the stock market, Buffett and Price take risks with their money. If forced to sell on the short-term, or during a bear market, they stand to lose a lot of money. Skittish investors put their money in safer bets, like buying gold, savings bonds, or bank certificates of deposit, rather than gamble it away on the stock market. But conservative investors like Buffett and Price show that a lower-risk, buy-and-hold approach can work for almost anybody. With a diverse portfolio and lots of patience, their stocks grew, sometimes slowly, but at a steady rate, making these men and their clients millionaires many times over.

On the other hand, aggressive investors treat the stock market like their own personal casinos. During the dot-com bubble of the 1990s and the highs of the mid-2000s, the stock market earned a reputation as a hip get-rich-quick opportunity. People quit their jobs to become day traders, some specializing in the short sale. In short selling, a trader sells stock, only to buy it back days or even minutes later, hoping to make a profit if the price drops. Day traders bet their money on short-term price movements that are almost impossible to predict with great accuracy. As stock guru Ralph Wanger once said, "If you believe you or anyone else has a system that can predict the future of the stock market, the joke is on you." Some day traders became wealthy, but most went broke, fast.

Perhaps some comfort to the average stockholder is that you can only lose what money you put in. Most people buy stocks with their

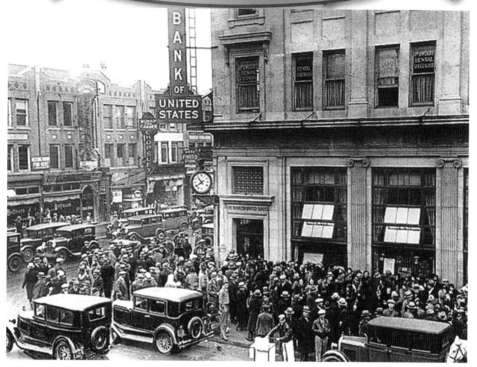

Nine thousand American banks closed their doors during the decade following 1929's Black Tuesday.

own money. It's risky business to buy stock on margin, which means you get a loan from a brokerage firm to buy more stocks. Margins help professional investors take advantage of a hot stock when cash is low. But if a stock's price drops, the pro gets hit twice. Not only is his investment money lost, but he also must pay back the money he borrowed. Brokers lent out margins as low as 10-to-1, or $9 on loan for every $1 already invested, before the stock market crash of 1929. On October 29, 1929, investors lost $14 billion (over $180 billion in modern cash value), when stocks plummeted. Investors couldn't pay back what they owed, and banks took anything they could to cover the debt, leaving the once-rich investors broke and even homeless. With over $14 billion evaporated in one day—and even more stock market losses to follow—this Black Tuesday marked for many the start of the Great Depression, a decade-long period of joblessness, homelessness, and hunger for many Americans.

CHAPTER 4

The chairman of the newly formed Securities and Exchange Commission, Joseph P. Kennedy (center), poses in 1934 with his Commissioners, (clockwise from bottom left) Ferdinand Pecora, George C. Matthews, Robert E. Healy, and James M. Landis.

As the first major crash of the US stock market, Black Tuesday taught the nation hard lessons. President Franklin D. Roosevelt created the Securities and Exchange Commission in 1934, in part to enforce stricter margin requirements to prevent another such disaster. Stock markets made rules that would halt trading when prices began to fall faster than a certain rate to limit panic selling. But even this added protection hasn't stopped crashes from recurring. Black Tuesday has nothing on October 19, 1987, a day that holds the record for the single largest drop in stock market history. The Dow Jones Industrial Average lost 22.6 percent; $1 trillion simply vanished from world stock exchanges. This Black Monday set off the bear market of the 1980s as cautious buyers kept stock prices low.

When the stock market drops, it's easy to get caught up in the selling panic. Inexperienced investors might think it best to sell their stock, to get out with at least some money while they still can. But savvy investors know that every company in their stock portfolio would have to go bankrupt for that to happen. They also know that, every few years, global stocks drop into a bear market where prices can stay low for a few months or years. In fact, if an average investor had bought stocks on January 2 of 1987 and then stayed put through Black Monday, they would have recovered all their losses by the year's end. The bear market of the late 1980s eventually gave way to a soaring rally in the late 1990s. Stocks climbed sharply on a "bubble" of excitement of IPOs

INVESTOR TRIVIA

In May 2012, the New York Stock Exchange created a new index that helped investors monitor the stock performance of 100+-year-old, US-based companies, called the Century Club. Each of the index's members must also have been publicly traded for at least ten years, and boast a market cap of at least $1 billion. In 2012, the index included 354 companies, such as:

Company	Symbol	In business since
Eli Lilly & Co.	LLY	1876
Ford Motor Co.	F	1903
Hershey	HSY	1894
Kimberly-Clark	KMB	1870
Kraft Foods	KRFT	1903
Macy's	M	1858
United Parcel Service	UPS	1907
Whirlpool	WHR	1908
Xerox	XRX	1906
*ConEdison	ED	1823

*Holds the record as the company with the longest continuous listing on the New York Stock Exchange.

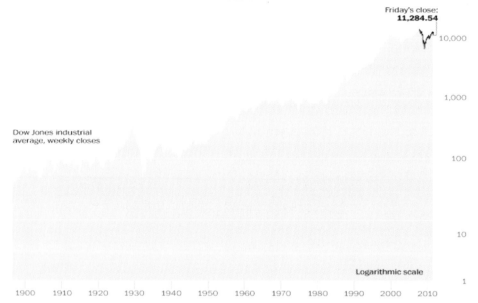

CHAPTER 5

Friday's close:
11,284.54

10,000

1,000

Dow Jones industrial
average, weekly closes

100

10

Logarithmic scale

1

1900   1910   1920   1930   1940   1950   1960   1970   1980   1990   2000   2010

The Dow Jones Industrial Average over time, in US dollars.

from new internet companies, or dot-coms, in 1996 and 1997. Investors rode the market to ever-increasing highs until the dot-com bubble burst between 2000 and 2002. Many dot-coms went belly up, leaving investors with worthless stock. Newly cautious investors brought on another bear market.

Dizzy yet from the cycles of market ups and downs? Wise investors never sell because of market swings. Despite market ups and downs over the past two decades, a recent Gallup poll reports that 54 percent of all Americans today own stock. An even greater percentage of college graduates and people with incomes of over $75,000 invest, 73 percent and 87 percent, respectively. These people have done their homework; they know that patience is key to success for the average investor. If you are in it for the long haul, investing to grow your money for college, or even for a comfortable retirement in fifty years, and if you don't mind a little risk, the stock market is the place for your money to be.

STOCKS TO EXPLORE

Company	Symbol	Industry	Sector	Market Cap
Conservative—Slower growing, less risk				
3M Company	MMM	Conglomerates	Conglomerates	73.07B
ConocoPhillips	COP	Basic Materials	Oil & Gas	74.33B
Heinz	HNZ	Food	Consumer Goods	23.09B
ExxonMobil	XOM	Basic Materials	Oil & Gas	23.09B
Johnson & Johnson	JNJ	Drug Manufacturers	Healthcare	222.47B
Kellogg	K	Packaged Foods	Consumer Goods	22.86B
Wells Fargo	WFC	Banking	Financial	196.64B
International Paper	IP	Paper & Paper Products	Consumer Goods	20.02B
IBM	IBM	Computers	Technology	236.98B
Southwest Airlines	LUV	Airlines	Services	9.19B
DuPont	DD	Chemicals	Materials	46.27B
Aggressive—Faster growing, more risk				
Apple	AAPL	Computers	Technology	429.00B
Target	TGT	Discount Stores	Services	44.25B
Caterpillar	CAT	Machinery	Industrial	57.09B
Comcast	CMCSA	CATV Systems	Services	108.25B
Costco	COST	Discount Stores	Services	45.57B
United Health	UNH	Healthcare Plans	Healthcare	55.97B
Panera Bread	PNRA	Specialty Eateries	Services	4.84B
Starbucks	SBUX	Specialty Eateries	Services	43.10B
FedEx	FDX	Freight	Services	30.91B

* These are not recommendations to purchase. Use this list to start your research into good stocks for your portfolio.

Bateman, Katherine R. *The Young Investor: Projects and Activities for Making Your Money Grow.* Chicago: Chicago Review Press, 2010.

Furgang, Kathy. *How the Stock Market Works.* New York: Rosen Publishing, 2011.

Gardner, David, Tom Gardner, and Selena Maranjian. *The Motley Fool Investment Guide for Teens: 8 Steps to Having More Money Than Your Parents Ever Dreamed Of.* New York: Fireside, 2002.

Lynch, Peter, and John Rothchild. *Learn to Earn: A Beginner's Guide to the Basics of Investing and Business.* New York: Simon & Schuster, 1996.

Roman, Rick. *I'm a Shareholder Kit: The Basics About Stocks—For Kids & Teens.* Gilbert, AZ: Leading Edge Gifts, 2012.

Thompson, Helen. *Understanding the Stock Market.* Broomall, PA: Mason Crest, 2009.

Investing Websites

Business News for Kids.
    http://www.businessnewsforkids.com/

IBFX: Teaching Kids About the Stock Market.
    https://www.ibfx.com/Education/Teaching-Kids-The-Stock-Market

Secret Millionaires Club.
    http://www.smckids.com/

TD Bank: Virtual Stock Market Game.
    http://virtualstockmarket.tdbank.com/

We Seed Virtual Stock Market Game.
    http://www.weseed.com/

Becket, Michael. *How the Stock Market Works: A Beginner's Guide to Investment.* Fourth Edition. London: KoganPage, 2012.

Ellyatt, Holly. " 'Black Monday': Could It Happen Again?" CNBC, October 19, 2012.

Frank, Robert, et. al. "Madoff Jailed After Admitting Epic Scam." *The Wall Street Journal,* March 13, 2009. http://online.wsj.com/article/SB1236856 93449906551.html?mod=djemalertNEWS

Healy, Paul M., and Krishna G. Palepu. "The Fall of Enron." *Journal of Economic Perspectives,* Vol. 17, No. 2, Spring 2003, pp. 3-26.

Investopedia. http://www.investopedia.com

Jacobe, Dennis. "In U.S., 54% Have Stock Market Investments, Lowest Since 1999." Gallup, April 20, 2011. http://www.gallup.com/poll/147206/stock-market-investments-lowest-1999.aspx

Kelly, Jason. *The Neatest Little Guide to Stock Market Investing.* New York: Penguin, 2008.

Lynch, Peter, and John Rothchild. *Learn to Earn: A Beginner's Guide to the Basics of Investing and Business.* New York: Simon & Schuster, 1996.

Mladjenovic, Paul. *Stock Investing For Dummies.* Third Edition. Hoboken, NJ: Wiley Publishing, Inc., 2009.

Page, Larry. "2012 Founders' Letter." From Google's Annual Report, issued December 31, 2011. http://investor.google.com/corporate/2012/founders-letter.html

Sander, Peter, and Scott Bobo. *The 100 Best Stocks You Can Buy 2012.* Avon, MA: Adams Media, 2011.

Sincere, Michael. *Understanding Stocks.* New York: McGraw-Hill, 2004.

The Motley Fool. http://www.fool.com

Tyson, Eric. *Investing For Dummies.* Fourth Edition. Hoboken, NJ: Wiley Publishing Inc., 2006.

United States Securities and Exchange Commission. "Investor.gov." http://www.investor.gov/

World Federation of Exchanges. "2012 WFE Market Highlights." January 22, 2013. http://www.world-exchanges.org/files/statistics/2012%20WFE%20Market%20Highlights.pdf

Yahoo! Finance. http://finance.yahoo.com

bear market—A prolonged period of falling stock prices, caused by cautious or pessimistic investors.

bull market—A prolonged period of rising stock prices, caused by aggressive or optimistic investors.

call option (KAWL OP-shuhn)—The option to buy a given stock before a given date at an agreed-upon price.

capital gains—Profit made from selling assets, such as stocks, bonds, or real estate.

common stock—A share of ownership in a corporation which offers voting rights; owners of this stock are the last to be paid in the event of a bankruptcy.

compound interest—Interest calculated on an original amount of money and any interest that money has already earned.

day trading—Buying and selling stocks on the short-term with the goal of making quick profits.

diversify (dih-VUR-suh-fahy)—To invest in different types of assets or at different times (in order to build a portfolio that protects an investor from large, sudden losses).

dividends (DIV-i-dendz)—Money paid to shareholders out of a corporation's earnings.

dollar-cost averaging—An investment strategy where money is invested in small amounts regularly over time.

earnings per share (EPS)—The net income of a corporation divided by the total number of shares of its common stock.

growth investing—An investment strategy to buy stock in corporations that are likely to grow over time.

initial public offering (IPO)—A corporation's first sale of shares to the public.

limit order—An order to buy or sell shares when they reach a certain price.

margin—Purchase of stock using borrowed money.

market capitalization (MAHR-kit kap-i-tul-uh-ZEY-shuhn)—The total value of all shares of a corporation's stock.

Ponzi scheme (PON-zee SKEEM)—An illegal investment operation that pays established investors by borrowing money from new investors.

price-to-earnings ratio (P/E ratio) (PRAHYS TOO UR-ningz REY-shee-oh)—The market price of a share of stock, divided by that corporation's annual earnings per share (EPS).

preferred stock—A share of ownership in a corporation that gives its owner a higher priority claim to the corporation's assets if it should go bankrupt.

put option (pooht OP-shuhn)—The option to sell a given stock before a given date at an agreed-upon price.

share—A portion of a corporation owned by a stockholder.

stock split—A change, usually an increase, in the number of shares of a corporation without a change in the total market capitalization of the corporation.

stop-loss order—An order to sell when a stock falls to a certain price, or to buy when it rises to a certain price; a stop-loss order protects sudden losses due to market swings.

value investing—An investment strategy to buy stock from undervalued companies and hold the stock for as long as possible.

volume (VOL-yoom)—Number of shares trading.

401(k)   29
Amazon.com   8–9, 13
Amsterdam Stock Exchange   6–7
Ann Taylor   28
annual report   22–27
Apple   15, 34
balance sheet   24–26
bear market   11, 29, 38, 40–41
    of the late 1980s   11, 40
    of 2000–2002   42
Bezos, Jeff   8-9
blue-chip stocks   28–29, 33
Buffett, Warren   36, 37–38
bull market   11, 41
Buttonwood Agreement   6
Calahan, Edward   32
capital gains   18–19
Century Club   41
Coca-Cola Corporation   32–35
common stock   15
compound interest   10–11
day trading   38
Di Modica, Arturo   11
diversification   27–28, 29
dividends   15, 18–19, 35
dot-com bubble   38, 41–42
Dow Jones Industrial Average (DJIA)   29, 33, 40, 42
Dutch East India Company   6–7
Dutch West India Company   7
earnings per share (EPS)   33, 34
Enron   26–27
Google   23–27, 34
Great Depression   39
income statement   24–25
initial public offering (IPO)   8–9, 41–42
Jamestown, Virginia   7
limit order   16
Lynch, Peter   21–22
Madoff, Bernie   19
margin trading   39, 40
market capitalization   27–28, 33, 41
market order   16
NASDAQ   8
New York Stock Exchange   4, 5–6, 8, 10, 20, 41
Nintendo Corporation   13, 22
Obama, Barack   36

online trading   14–15
options   16–18
Page, Larry   23
PepsiCo   32–35
Ponzi scheme   19
portfolio   22, 27–29, 38, 40, 43
    monitoring 31–35
preferred stock   15
price-to-earnings (P/E) ratio   33, 34, 37
rate of return   9–11
Roosevelt, Franklin D.   40
Securities and Exchange Commission   22, 25, 26, 40
shareholders' equity   26
short sale   38
Smith, John   7
S&P 500   29, 37–38
stockbroker   5-6, 13–17, 19, 32, 38, 39
stock certificate   13, 14
stock investment strategies
    buying and selling   13–18
    choosing stocks   21–29
    dollar-cost averaging   29
    growth investing   38
    online research   14–15, 31–35
    value investing   37–38
    young people and   10–11, 42
stock market crashes
    Black Monday, the crash of 1987   40, 41
    Black Tuesday, the Wall Street Crash of 1929   39–40
stock markets
    history of   6–8
    international   8
stock split   23-24
stock statistics   31-35, 37–38
stop-loss order   16
taxes   18–19
ticker symbol   32, 35
Tontine Coffee House   6
Virginia Company of London   7–8
Wall Street   5–6, 8, 11
The Wall Street Journal   29, 31
Wanger, Ralph   38
WorldCom   26–27

About the
AUTHOR

Claire O'Neal has written over two dozen books for Mitchell
Lane. She holds degrees in English and Biology from Indiana
University, and a Ph.D. in Chemistry from the University of
Washington. Claire lives in Delaware—home of tax-free shopping
—where she and her husband use their stock-market wizardry to
grow investment accounts in the hopes of a cozy beachfront
retirement. Claire also balances her checkbook for fun.